Evincepub
Publishing

LITEROMA

*Feel The Difference*

# Evincepub Publishing

Nehru Nagar, Bilaspur, Chhattisgarh 495001
First Published by Evincepub Publishing 2021
Copyright © Rakhi Sameer 2021
All Rights Reserved.

**ISBN: 9789354460838**

## Disclaimer

# Psychology of Money

By

## Dr. Rakhi Sameer

COVER DESIGN BY:

LITEROMA

# ABOUT THE AUTHOR

Rakhi Sameer is  an Internationally Accredited life and Relationship Coach . She has several dimensions to her diverse and dynamic personality . She has been a college lecturer, a Corporate Trainer. Is also a Feng Shui master. Dr Rakhi is a prolific writer. And a life Coach .
Contact her: rmsameer10@gmail.com

# PREFACE

Money is an integral part of our lives. It is important that we have a healthy relationship with money. We need to ascertain what drives our behaviour concerning money. We all have a unique relationship with money, this is determined by a host of attitudes, opinions and also past experiences. These and several other factors predispose us to living a life in a way where money works in a positive way to achieve our goals.

On the surface, money is just a physical bill or a few coins....but the emotion humans attach to it make it most significant thing in our lives. Most of our emotional connection to money is grounded in our memories from childhood, and we are mostly not conscious or aware that our money history is playing a role in it. We all should actually take a journey down our own money history, and examine how that shaped our experiences related to money. We may discover and even identify variety of responses that we habitually have towards money, like hoarding ,anxiety, guilt, fear that are probably a part of your money history.

An understanding of these things may help you build a capability to bring about a shift in your thoughts and feelings leading to a better relationship with money.

"If we command our wealth, we shall be rich and free.If our wealth commands us , we are poor indeed." Edmund Burke.

# TABLE OF CONTENTS

# *Introduction*

———•———

Money can be something that excites, scares, intimidates or empowers us. Our perception and understanding of money starts at a young age as we watch our parents handle it. As we get older, it is compounded by our own experiences with money. Whether we grow up with money or without it, whether money is a source of freedom or stress, every interaction and experience that we have with money and wealth as we grow up influences the subconscious beliefs that we hold about it as adults. It is these beliefs that can dramatically impact our finances, both positively and negatively, in terms of our ability to earn, hold and grow money.

As human beings, we tend to devote our energy to things that interest us and give us pleasure, and we tend to procrastinate on and avoid things we find challenging or don't like. If we see money positively, as a tool that can be utilised to build a happy life and give back to our community, then we tend to pay attention to it and try to accumulate it. However, if our experience of money involves stress, challenges or confusion, it makes sense that we're not going out of our way to devote any more energy to it than we absolutely have to. It's not a coincidence that many people who aren't happy with their financial situation also hate managing their money. Whether they think money isn't important or that only greedy people have surplus money in the bank, their negative perspective on all things financial means that they tend to focus on other, more enjoyable things and hope that their money just takes care of itself.

Money is like a drug, when viewed in the psychological sense of the word. We all desire to have money, although the degree may vary from person to person and society to society. Money is a tool; we can use it in various ways. Money yields power. Money also has power over us.

We place a lot of importance on money, yet most of us do not know much about what we personally believe about money and the relationship we have with it.

Exploring our relationship with money — and learning to resolve the problematic areas in that relationship — can make a significant improvement in our financial well-being. Yet, just as often as we do with other vital financial actions like drafting wills, we tend to avoid looking at our beliefs about money.

Money is an important part of life; it affects all areas of our lives, either directly or indirectly.

Money affects our relationships, career choices, education and almost all other things. However, what is most important is our attitude towards money. How do we feel about money? What thoughts come to mind when we think about money? How do we use money? And, most importantly, why do we have the attitude that we have towards money?

**Understanding our relationship with money is essential because it will govern how money presents itself in our life.** It is a deeply emotional connection, which we aren't even aware of until we open up the layers and find the underlying beliefs that give birth to the feelings governing our relationship with money.

We need to understand the meaning of 'relationship' in this context. According to the dictionary, the definition of 'relationship' is 'the way in which two or more people or things are connected.'

**How do we connect with our money?**

When we think about our relationships with people, we know whether it's a good relationship, a difficult one or even a bad one. Is it a close connection or a distant one? Then, there are the emotions attached to them. The good relationships, for example, probably make us feel happy, loved and secure. We love to be around such people, whereas the difficult ones arouse emotions like anger, jealousy or even fear. But when it comes to money, **many of us don't even give it a second thought.** We're not used to thinking of money in terms of a relationship, and because of that, most of the time there is no thought given to what is our relationship with money.

Money is an integral part of our lives; we interact with it many times a day. Therefore, it is important that our relationship with money is a healthy one because **if we have a dysfunctional relationship with money, it will impact not just our financial well-being, but our whole life.**

What are the first five words that come to our mind when we hear the word 'money?' Try asking this of people; almost every word that we will get will be negative. Generally, we all have similar feelings for money. These words may include 'stressful,' 'elusive' and 'complicated.'

We have to understand our financial situation is not going to change unless our attitude towards money changes. The most empowering thing about this realisation is the understanding that we actually have control over our situation. We can change our attitude, find reasons to get excited about money, and, in the process, we can turn our financial future around. Rather than seeing wealth as unnecessary and a burden, we can start to think of it as something that will allow us to make a real difference in the world.

Everyone has a complex relationship with money. How we acquire, spend, and manage money is largely due to two factors: our early childhood, what we observed about money, the values related to it and the way we organised this information in our minds. For example, if we value religion, we might like to give away money to a religious organisation. Or, if we value education, we may prioritise college savings.

This relationship with money lies on a spectrum. Financial insecurity lies on either end of this spectrum. At one end, we may be extremely frugal and uptight due to relative scarcity and dearth of means. Whereas, at the other hand, we may be irresponsible and reckless. The way we process or develop and organise money messages or information along with the way in which we model money behaviours is unique to each individual. If you think about it, the concept of money is quite vague. We think we have money in the bank, but actually it is not there. Once we deposit our money in the bank, the bank lends it to someone else. So, physically the money isn't there.

All that exists are numbers that we check on our smartphone.

We trust the systems that operate around us. We trust that our money is in the bank, and the bank will give it back to us whenever we ask for it. We feel safe and secure in the knowledge that our money is in the bank.

We are profoundly psychological beings. We are whatever is in our minds. Money, too, is a mental construct. It is an idea, but an idea on which we depend to procure most of the things that we need to live.

Money has an extraordinary power over our mind. It gives us a promise of the things we value. It promises us a whole lot of things that we need in life. Here is something that is abstract and virtual, a product of our minds, which helps us create the things we need and want.

We read a lot about consumerism and capitalism and the evils of money. Or what to do with money or how to make it. Different people approach the topic of money from different perspectives.

The psychologist Freud compared money to faeces, saying children are initially interested in playing with their waste products before they move onto need, then stores and eventually money.

The nineteenth century philosopher and psychologist William James thought of money as our extended self. The historian Yuval Noah Harari calls money the "most universal and most efficient system."

All our lives are spent studying; we work hard throughout our lives and pay taxes. After having paid the bills and taxes, at the end of the month, we are left with very little. We have so many loans to pay, credit card bills to pay — all this is an enormous burden. It appears as if we never have enough for us to spend. We need the latest phone, latest cars, and televisions. We want to travel the world. We have friends who have all of this. Then, we have this huge sense of 'missing out.' And when we see our friends who have all these things, we get upset, frustrated and sad. There are people around us who have all the privileges. Someone will always be better than us. Even though we work very hard, we never seem to have enough. Something is not right somewhere.

# Chapter I
## Uses of Money

———◆———

*"Money can't buy love, but it improves your bargaining position."*

People often think they are not being treated fairly, and they also feel that everyone cannot have everything. If others have a lot of money, it does not mean that they are depriving us of money. By thinking like this, we attach a lot of negative emotions to money. We think as if there is scarcity in the world; if someone else has what we want, we cannot have it. We live in this scarcity mindset. Hence, we get insecure, fearful and jealous. This thinking never helps us. Thinking like this, we will always be lacking and feeling deprived. Because there will always be something bigger, better and more desirable, if we don't have that, we will feel left out. This becomes an endless cycle that will keep us trapped in a never-ending process of accumulation.

To come out of this internal condition of scarcity that gives rise to greed, jealousy and prejudice, we will have to get rid of the idea of scarcity, that mindset of scarcity. We have to stop thinking that things aren't fair. We will have to stop looking at what we don't have and start looking at what we have. We have a house. We have clothes. We have a car. But, our neighbours have better and more expensive cars, houses and clothes. They are richer. They are better off. They have taken your share of things.

## What are the benefits of money?

Does money really help us with whatever we want to do in life?
Is it because of money we are unable to achieve our dreams?
Do you think money likes you? Do you like money? Are your money stories similar to the money stories of your parents?

Money projects various feelings in different people. We make money an easy target for our resentments and jealousies, and blame money for all the evils of humanity. A simple object, yet it holds a lot of responsibility. So, is money the problem....or are we the problem?

You will have to analyse what your relationship with money is. What are the feelings you project? What are the feelings that money arouses in you? For some people, money creates a sense of security; for others it means freedom — freedom to choose, act, behave and think. Some people use it to control; to them it may mean power.

You need to check which feeling it arouses in you. You will have to recognise the emotion you get from money. This is not going to be an easy exercise. It requires a lot of introspection and clarity. You will have to go deep into your beliefs and values, and find out how you developed these beliefs. And finally unearth what money means to you.

Our feelings towards money are never very clear. This makes us feel that life is unfair. We feel unworthy and diminished. We always live with this feeling that others have more than us. Most of these feelings begin from the utility value of money or the function that money provides. Broadly speaking, the function of money can be classed into three categories:

**Barter**

We can use money as barter, the original function of money. We use money in exchange for something—it could be food, land, clothes, grain or medical help—anything. This kind of use gives it power because when we have money, we feel we can have anything we want.

When we do not have money, we feel powerless. This causes stress and the fear that when we need something, we will not be able to get it.

**Saving**

Primitive man hunted animals for food. They ate as much as they could and then looked for ways to store it or find ways to use the remaining parts before it began to rot. The aim was to prevent weeks' worth of chasing and hunting animals to go to waste. Hence, in order to preserve the value of their work, they want to save or use up their kill. This same primitive instinct exists even today. We want to retain the value of our hard work. We spend what we have to spend and save the rest. We may want to put it in bank. Not just save, we also want our money to grow.

After working year after year throughout life, we want to have something to show for it. We think this is our life's worth.

## Grow

We want our money to grow. We expect to gain interest on what we deposit at the bank. People who already have money keep growing it. The rich will keep getting richer. The poor or those with little money will continue to feel inadequate.

## We all want money

Everyone, rich or poor, wants money. People spend their entire lives wanting to earn more and more.

If you ask someone what they want most, most people will say money. They may not know for sure what they need it for. Why do we always want money? What is that motivating factor for us to want money so badly? Are there any emotional reasons for the desire to earn more and more money? Do we even understand the real reason behind our desire to have money? If we can somehow have clarity on that, we will have a better perspective for our emotional reasons for wanting money. Maybe we will start feeling more connected to our own self, our needs and then maybe we will feel less stressed about money.

In people's desire to have money, a pattern can be seen. Let's have a look at some of these patterns:

#Enables a lifestyle

We all have certain basic needs like food, house and clothes to exist. Whatever we need in our life can be bought with money. So, most, or rather all, of us need money to lead the kind of life we want to live.

#Power

Money gives you power to control people. If you have money, you can make people do things for you. That is why rich people are considered powerful. This emotion is negative and addictive as well, and it blocks true happiness from your life.

Most politicians are hungry and greedy for money; however, after attaining a lot of wealth, they get hungry for power and control.

Very often, when we embark on the journey of financial planning, we get caught up in the process and forget the purpose. A too-tight focus on money and its care has the potential to leach away the joy that money can bring. Equally, on the other hand, a too-tight focus on instant gratification has the potential to reduce us to our baser instincts. We must reconnect with the deeper meaning of money in our lives, discover our relationship with money and then if we don't like what we find, change it to what the aspiration is.

For us to discover our relationship with money, we should be able to explore all the insecurities, emotions and experiences that having or not having money have brought into our lives till now. This is not easy to do since the energy of money is acutely entangled with every aspect of our lives such that it is difficult to unriddle the real reason for doing what we do. It helps to see this through three lenses—how we earn, spend and look after money.

It matters how we earn this money. With what intention do you do what you do and then get compensated for your labour makes the difference between just doing a job, running a business or spending the productive years of life in some meaningful work. There is always a choice and you can choose the one with more meaning rather than the one with more money. There are times in life when money without meaning is needed, and it is fine to do that, but never let the flame of meaning die out. Money that comes due to meaning in work has a different flavour. Savour it.

It matters how we spend this money. The day we find out why we spend the way we spend, we have the key to our relationship with money. We spend for different reasons — to assuage that guilt in our heart for not spending time with our kids, to quell the insecurity that, as a child, we carried around because our parents could not send us for a school trip that everybody was going for, or to show our peer group that we have arrived by buying an expensive car. We may also spend on expensive birthday gifts to get over a decaying relationship, or to celebrate a milestone together, or even to enjoy a trip.

Is it brand over comfort or is it need over greed? A good way to work through your own relationship with money is to watch yourself educating your child on money. Then watch what you do yourselves — saying very high-sounding things but may be doing the opposite. Saying and doing are often not the same. Find out why you spend (or don't spend), and life is never the same again. It matters how we look after this money. Fear, panic, confusion and greed are the typical emotions we feel when we think of looking after our money.

**Why do people want money?**

We all want money. Everyone, whether rich or poor, wants money. Generally, if we ask people they would say they want money for food. We must recognise that there is a difference between basic needs and what we consider luxury.

There are several people who earn fairly good salaries to take care of the basic needs of the family. Despite that, they always feel that they are not earning enough. If you look at how they spend their money, they have a reasonably good house — the best that they can afford, and a good car. A large amount of their monthly income is spent on food and entertainment.

# Chapter II

## Money Personality

––––•––––

Our emotional reaction to money is significant and essential to understand our relationship with money. This is known as money EQ, which includes how we receive, enjoy and share our money. It also shows how confident we feel about money.

A pattern can be seen in our relationship with money. If we ascertain the money pattern of our personality, we can have a healthier relationship with money. We need to first find out our present equation with money. We also need to find out how we got there. We will have to explore the history of our family. Explore stories about our parents and sometimes, our grandparents as well. Exploring our roots is important to understand ourselves better. If we have a greater understanding of our descent, it becomes easier to reprogram our mindset, values and beliefs.

Our money personalities are deeply related to how we were raised. But, is it possible to move past our beliefs around money? Can we move past our current mental blocks? Can we move past our emotions in our relationship with money?

There are several money personalities. Let us discuss these in some detail.

## The Saver

These people love to save money. They are capable of finding innovative ways of saving money. Even if they get a small amount, they will try and save it. Saving money gives them a sense of security.

They hate to spend; they would only like to save. They have exceptional bargaining skills. They can probably tell you about different sales and discounts in town. They are happiest checking their savings account and seeing it grow.

Such people do not like to spend on their hobbies or even on any customary activities. If you ask them, they probably will have little or no clue at all why they became such a big hoarder or collector.

However, realistically speaking, there is a backstory to these compulsive or obsessive savers. They probably grew up in families without much money and must have suffered several dreadful experiences in their childhood. For some reason, their parents never had enough money—maybe they went bankrupt or lost their jobs, or were not able to earn enough for the family.

These individuals suffered from a lack of money in their childhood. They are very anxious about money. Their anxiety is not erased no matter how much they save. They need to confront their fears and anxieties about money and delve deeper. They will always have a fear of running out of money.

Such savers are people who think ahead. While they can live and enjoy the moment, they are always stressed about money. If you tend to be a hoarder, you like to save money. You also like to prioritise your financial goals. You probably have a budget and may enjoy the processes of making up a budget and reviewing it periodically. You most likely have a hard time spending money on yourself and your loved ones for luxury items or even practical gifts. These purchases seem frivolous to you. You might very well view spending money on entertainment and on vacations—and even on clothing—as largely unnecessary expenses. If you think about investing your money, you tend to be concerned not with liquidity but with future security, especially during retirement. 'Saving for a rainy day' appeals to your orderly nature. If you are an extreme hoarder, you may want to keep your money so close to you that you avoid putting it even in conservative investments such as money markets, bonds or mutual funds. Some hoarders have been known to keep their money hidden under mattresses and in other secret places rather than put it in a bank. However, these cases are relatively rare. Depending on how extreme your hoarder tendencies are, you might exhibit some, most, or all of these traits.

Overall, a saver is someone who is excellent with budgeting as well as living within their means. If you ever go on a group vacation, you should put a saver in charge of the money because he or she is going to make sure that you'll stay within your budget while having a good time.

Most people assume that it is better to be a saver. After all, if we can live comfortably while keeping some money for the future, that will pay off a lot better than being a spender. On the surface, that is undoubtedly the case, but being a saver is not without its downsides.

In more extreme cases, savers can have much anxiety when it comes to spending money. They don't like to do so unless it's absolutely necessary, and parting with the money they've worked so hard to can be difficult at times.

The other disadvantage is that they can be seen as cheap by others, particularly spenders. While they see the value in delayed gratification, others may think that they're too tight or rigid with their money. After all, life is for living, right?

Savers are also much more patient. They are good at setting financial goals and working towards them. However, in some instances, if something derails those goals (i.e., a major unexpected expense), it can have an adverse impact on them as well.

For the most part, people can pretty much tell whether they're a saver or a spender, but if you want to be sure, then here are a few ways to know if saving is in your blood:

- You feel good when saving money. Seeing your accounts grow over time fills you with pride as you contribute more and more into those funds.

- You tend to think more about the future and retirement. You feel more confident about the future when you're able to save more than you thought you would.

- You live within your means. If you can't afford something right now, you wait until you have the money to buy it.

- You have no problem curtailing to save more. If necessary, you  can abstain from most luxuries, especially when you have to reach a financial goal or you want to save for something in particular (e.g., a vacation).

- You are detailed and organised, particularly with your finances. Not just that, you feel much better when everything is laid out neatly and in order.

The most notable aspect of being a saver is that they take more pleasure in earned purchases, rather than impulse buys. If they have saved money for a new car, for example, they feel much better about getting it than they would if they put it on credit or bought it without going over the financials and the options available.

## The Spender

On the opposite end of the spectrum, we have spenders. Unlike savers, they are more concerned about living in the moment and not necessarily planning for the future. While most spenders are not out of control with their spending habits, they value what's happening now over what's going to happen tomorrow.

In the group vacation scenario, we may not want to put a spender in charge of the budget. Yes, we'll have a great time and do some incredible things, but we may have to cut our vacation short because we ran out of funds too fast.

Spenders are usually more outgoing and see money as a means to an end.

*"I'm buying this thing because I want it."*

*"I'm going out to eat because I'm craving this type of food."*

Instead of seeing the intrinsic value of money, they think about it in terms of what it can be used for.

Overall, spenders are not that great with budgeting, but they are fun to hang out with. At the bar, they're more concerned with the great feeling that comes from buying drinks for their friends than they are with the bill that's going to come at the end.

The other side of being a spender is that it can create anxiety when the other shoe drops. Yes, they engaged in instant gratification, but it could wind up costing them more than they expected in the long run. Usually, spenders find it easy to get into debt, but really hard to get out. In many cases, they may end up living beyond their means.

The spenders love to spend. Whenever they find some money, they will instantly buy something or the other. It's great to have compulsive spenders as friends; their motto is that you only live once. These people are usually very amicable and affable. They love showering their friends with gifts.

The spenders spend money because it makes them feel more in control. When they buy something, they get some level of control over their surroundings.

**Traits of a spender**

Once again, you should already have an idea of the type of financial personality you embody, but here are some ways that you can be sure you're a spender.

- You dip into your savings more often than you contribute to it. In some instances, you may not even have savings.

- If you get a raise or a bonus, you think about what you can buy with the money, not how much of it you can save.

- You're susceptible to impulse buys on a regular basis. You've certainly had buyer's remorse more than a few times.

- You're not too concerned about putting things on credit. The concept of 'buy now, pay later' speaks to you on a deeper level.

- When you go out to eat, you focus more on what looks good, not the price.

- When you think about your next vacation, you consider what's going to be the most fun rather than what your budget will be.

- You can usually set financial goals, but they often take much longer to happen than you anticipate.

Because spenders are the opposite of savers, they focus more on living in the moment. The idea of delayed gratification seems like too much of a downer. In some cases, spenders may be able to stick to a budget if they're sufficiently motivated, but they can't go too long without splurging a little.

## The Indifferent-to-Money Type

These people are totally indifferent to the existence of money. They hardly realise that money exists. If they see some money lying on street, they will ignore it and move ahead. Typically, we find such people in teachers, professors, doctors, artists and homemakers. They keep moving on with life without being much aware of money. They usually have their partner or spouse managing their finances for them, to the extent that they do not even know properly how much they really have in terms of money, or for that matter where their financial documents are. They are really not concerned. The reason for this could be that they are well-off. As a child they were well taken care of, and they did not think much about money. Such people are generally happy people.

## People who think money is bad

Yes, there are people who think money is bad. If they find some money, they instinctively give it to a charity. They do not feel right spending it on themselves.

For such people, money is a problem. They are least affected by money.

If you are a money monk, you think that money is dirty and bad, and that if you have too much of it, it will corrupt you. In general, such people believe that 'money is the root of all evil.' It stands to reason that they identify with people of modest means rather than those who amass wealth. If they happen to come into a fortune somehow (through inheritance, for example), they tend to be uneasy and even very anxious at the thought of the influx of so much money. They worry that they might 'sell out,' become greedier and more selfish, and lose sight of positive human, political and/or spiritual ideals and values. They probably avoid investing their money for fear that it might grow and make them even wealthier. If they were willing to invest some of it, they would most likely be comfortable only with socially responsible investments that reflected their deeper values and convictions and contribute to causes they would like to support.

**The Gambler**

They inherently like excitement, fun and thrill. They are ready to take risks, but they are not good losers—they like to win. They enjoy the thrill of winning. They enjoy the high of the thought of winning, but they may not always win. Consequently, such people can suffer major and devastating losses or even have windfalls of profits. These people are gamblers in the true sense of the word. They cannot lead a monotonous life. They would rather die than live a life of monotony. It's seen that mostly one of their parents was a saver. They get bored of living with a parent who is always tight on money. As a reaction to that boredom, they become gamblers or spenders.

# *Chapter III*

## **Money Anxiety**

We now know that the way we were raised determines what kind of money personality we become. So, is there are a way to move forward from this behaviour that limits us or our beliefs that determine our money personality? Is there a way to overcome our current blocks?

To get rid of our pre-set notions about money, we need to have a better understanding of our present blocks that restrain us from entering our present world. There are several mental blocks that we carry from our childhood.

To create prosperity, it is very, very important to understand what is our relationship with money.

What concepts and attitudes about money and wealth have we learned from our parents, our community and our culture? Most certainly, our upbringing and our early years environment has shaped our view of ourselves and our attitude towards money and other things in life. But that does not necessarily mean that we have caged ourself into that mindset about money.

Each of us carries conscious and unconscious beliefs about ourselves, and about what we can expect to achieve from childhood into adulthood. Therefore, to have a positive change in our relationship with money, it is important that we have a clear picture of who we are, where we are from, and where we want to be. When we have clarity about ourself, only then can we move towards our financial goals. We can make conscious choices that lead to our financial goals.

A lot of people fear change. We fear losing friendships and love, and we fear loss. Because of our inherent fear of loss, we put in a great deal of effort into managing our risk of loss. Another overwhelming feeling is that of anxiety. Anxiety is the discomfort and uneasiness experienced when either taking or planning an action. Anxiety is also an indicator that change is near. Anxiety can also be indicative of our more deep-seated fears. So, if we get anxious and fearful about money, there needs to be a deeper cause.

## Causes of money anxiety

Feeling anxious about money is a perfectly rational response in certain situations. For example, if we've recently lost our job or our employer has announced a coming round of layoffs, it's natural to be concerned about our financial future and how we'll make ends meet. If we have a healthy relationship with money, however, these worries won't be paralysing, and will pass when the problem does. But when our money anxiety gets out of hand, it can cause behaviours that prevent us from making the most of our money and may even cause us financial harm.

Actions often linked to money anxiety include:

- **Overspending**: If we regularly use shopping as a way to relieve stress, we might go on a spending spree to relieve our anxiety about money. Unfortunately, this is a vicious circle because spending too much will only serve to worsen our money stress.

- **Hoarding**: While some people overspend, others hoard money. They may feel like they never have enough, and may become workaholics in their need to have more and more money. This can mean less time spent with their family and on their own, which can take a mental toll.

- **Excessive frugality**: Being penny-wise can help us avoid unnecessary spending and build up savings, but it's possible to take frugality too far. If you find it difficult to spend money even on necessities, such as critical home repairs or dental visits, you might be suffering from money anxiety.

• **Dysfunctional family finances**: The way your family deals with money can also reflect or cause money anxiety. For example, a partner may handle all the finances and use money to control the other. Parents may enable their adult children by supporting them financially, removing the child's motivation to become independent. Couples sometimes hide their purchasing habits from each other, run up credit card debt without telling their partners, or even maintain secret bank accounts.

When we suffer from money anxiety, it can feel like the stress will never end. But taking a few basic steps, such as setting a budget, building an emergency fund and monitoring our credit score, we can reset our attitude to money. By taking charge of our finances, we can shake off money stress and start down the path toward achieving our financial goals.

**Four basic steps to deal with money anxiety**

**1. Pay attention to the signs and acknowledge its presence**

Be it a medical, psychological or financial problem, the first step of fixing anything is always understanding the problem (here, money anxiety) and identifying its causes. While this introspection can be stressful in itself, we need to tell ourself that it is the only thing that will get us out of anxiety.

## 2. Plan finances well

After introspecting and understanding where our anxiety is coming from, nail the hammer on the head. Getting a financial plan in place will play a major role in initiating a stress-free state of mind. For most people, the worry stems from the fear of not meeting financial goals. All of this can be avoided by planning our finances.

There are many ways of going about planning. The most basic one includes creating a budget. This entails calculating and adding up all our sources of income and then subtracting all our monthly dues including debt, taxes, EMI(s), etc. Once we have done this, we will get a fair idea of our financial standing.

Invest in healthy and safe luxuries as and when the budget allows. Stringent saving plans might mentally frustrate us.

## 3. Manage debt efficiently

Most people who are in debt are likely to be suffering from money anxiety. Sometimes, it's also the fear of getting into debt that causes anxiety. Either way, debt can be avoided with a strong financial plan in place.

The idea is not to get rid of debt the next day, but it is to know that we are making some progress on it by the day. We need to list our debts and prioritise them. Next, we need to set in motion a plan that helps us pay off our debts slowly.

If we are not in debt currently, but fear that we soon will be, planning is the key again. Plan for emergencies by setting up an emergency fund. In this way, we know that we have secured ourself financially for any emergency that poses a risk of debt.

**4. Give your mental space some rest**

Sometimes, we might be doing everything right and yet feel stressed. That's because we humans often let our mind give in to worry, even when things are fine. It is also likely that we might be feeling lost because we feel we don't entirely understand where we are headed financially. It is always a good idea to unburden ourself by talking to someone about our financial worries. We can confide in our family, relatives, friends or even professional financial advisors.

Money and finances are two things that we can never know enough about. Being stressed or anxious about money is normal. Moreover, one can easily get rid of money-related anxiety.

# *Chapter IV*

## Can Money Buy Happiness?

————◆————

We often hear people say that money can't buy happiness. If that's true, then why is everybody chasing money? Why do people want money so desperately? Why do people become criminals for money?

The reason that money increases happiness up to a point seems to be that having a certain amount of money helps fix certain problems in life that make people stressed out and unhappy. If our car breaks down and we don't have enough money to fix it, that can be stressful. If we have a health problem and not enough money, we have two sets of worries—our health and our money. If we get divorced and there's not enough money for legal costs and keeping up two houses, the financial issues make the breakup worse than it would otherwise be.

So, it's not necessarily money that makes people happy. More than that, money can help to solve problems that would otherwise reduce their happiness.

Why do we want financial freedom? Why is financial freedom so important to us? How will financial freedom change or transform our life?

My initial answer to this question has always been to spend time with family and friends and to do the things I really enjoy doing.

While my reasons remain true now, they are not powerful enough to motivate me for the long term.

Seeking financial freedom is like climbing a high mountain slowly. There are challenges all along the way. There is a need to find the true motivation that is sustainable and will get us through the campaign to the top of that mountain to accomplish the eventual objective of financial freedom.

**More than just financial freedom, it's our life's purpose that's the real reason behind the sacrifices we make to climb that mountain and reach our ultimate goal of financial freedom.**

WHY to climb this mountain is our purpose.

It steers us in the right direction. It directs our actions to success. It tells us the skills that we must acquire. It gives us the long-term motivation we require. It gives us the persistence and perseverance to overcome all obstacles.

Ask the WHY question like a three-year-old more than eight times and you will uncover your life's purpose. Continuously respond to each question with the question, "*Why [insert your previous answer here]?"* until you get to your life's purpose; your 'foundational' WHY.

Here's one example:

(1) Why do you get out of bed this morning? So that I can go to work.

(2) Why do you go to work? So that I can earn money.

(3) Why do you want to earn money? So that I can put food on the table and invest for the future.

(4) Why do you want to invest for the future? So that I can be financially free, to spend more time with my family, to volunteer and not worry about money when I retire. I invest time in building a business that will generate passive income for me in the future. I invest time in accumulating the right knowledge and skills. I invest money in income-producing assets.
Most people will stop here. While this can be powerful, it's not powerful enough to keep me going for the long term.
Success is like running a marathon. It's not a sprint. Success takes time and significant effort over the long term. It's not a get-rich-quick scheme. There are no new shining objects to chase.

But the question remains: can money buy happiness?

Money is important to happiness. Ask anyone who doesn't have it. Having a higher income, for example, can give us access to homes in safer neighbourhoods, better health care and nutrition, fulfilling work and more leisure time. However, this only works up to a certain point. Once our income reaches a certain level and our basic needs for food, health care, safety and shelter are met, the positive effects of money — such as buying your dream home — are often offset by the negative effects — such as working longer hours or in more stressful jobs to maintain that income.

Most people assume that 'things' will lead to more happiness than 'experiences.' Physical objects — such as the latest iPhone, handbag, or car — last longer than going to a concert, taking a cooking class or going on a vacation. Buying things does make us happy, at least in the short term. In the long term, however, we become habituated to new things and even though they make us excited and happy at first, eventually the item becomes the new normal and fades into the background. The happiness that comes from purchasing experiences, however, tends to increase over time. One reason is that we often share experiential purchases with other people. Even when we've driven that new car into the ground, we'll still be telling stories to family and friends about that time when we went on a vacation to Europe and we'll even be laughing about the time when the car broke down and we had to spend the night in a shady hotel.

That can be fulfilling. That can be incredibly satisfying. That's our life's purpose.

We are all told and we believe that the most basic form of success is to make the next generation's life better. If we are lucky, our parents must have worked hard to successfully create a better (and easier) life for us. In return, we would like to pass on that same legacy to our children.

Firstly, we want to future-proof our income and achieve a state of financial well-being before it's too late. We want to protect and secure our income in preparation for the future and address the challenges of work, finances and technology. It's our contingency plan for retirement. We want to live a life of financial independence and security, doing the things that we want with the resources that we have.

Secondly, in future-proofing our income, we also want to build a solid foundation upon which our children can live a life to their full potential and be financially free themselves doing the things that they want in the earlier part of their lives. The knowledge that we have gathered for ourselves to secure and protect our own income will also be useful in guiding our children through life's challenges in preparation for their future.

As a responsible parent, we want to set them up for future success. We want to help them overcome the challenges of today's life and the challenging world of work, economics and technological innovation. The world is moving so quickly that we need to keep up with it ourself. In doing so, we can use the same information to help our children navigate these same challenges and build a solid foundation upon which their financial well-being can also be taken care of.

This is why we wake up, go to work, earn money, invest for the future, and create financial freedom for ourselves so that we can achieve the state of financial well-being.

Financial freedom or financial well-being is a means to an end. The end for us is the achievement of our life's purpose. The existence of more money will give us the freedom we need to fund our life's purpose, to have full control over our finances, and to have the freedom to make choices that will allow us to enjoy life with our family.

**What's your life's purpose that will ultimately drive your WHY and desire to make more money for yourself?**

Just earning more money without a strong underlying WHY will not inspire anyone to start and succeed in 10 to 20 years' time. Knowing that we are getting closer to achieving our life's purpose every day, bit-by-bit will motivate us to keep doing the things that we are currently doing and to persistently overcome challenges.

Most people think that spending money on themselves will make them happier than spending it on other people. Yet, when researchers assess happiness before and after people spend an annual bonus, people report greater happiness when they spend the bonus money on others or donate it to charity than when they spend it on themselves. This occurs regardless of how big the bonus was. One reason for this phenomenon is that giving to others makes us feel good about ourselves.

Happiness in a way does not depend on a person's absolute income level, but on their relative position in society, i.e., whether they have more or less than their peers. There is an assumption that raising the income of the poorest would clearly have a significant impact on their quality of life and overall happiness.

Some studies have found that people at higher income levels are more satisfied with life. There is no point of saturation, a higher income equals more happiness at all levels. These studies even showed that where incomes are increased by the same percentage, the impact is stronger at higher income levels than at lower income levels.

However, there are numerous aspects of life that are not directly related to money. People may suffer from illnesses or break-ups at any income level. Although, it is seen that poor people also experience adverse circumstances e.g., illness, divorce or loneliness as inexorably worse than their more affluent counterparts. This estimation is all the more important as it shows that income and wealth affect other areas of life as well.

Whenever someone says that money is not important or even that money makes you unhappy, their aim is obvious. As they have no money, their words are devised to bring solace to themselves.

The vast majority of people, however, would certainly agree that freedom makes people happy. And far fewer people would dare to argue with the fact that 'freedom' is clearly positive and desirable than would reject the notion that money is something positive and desirable. But financial freedom is an important component of freedom in general. Only the financially free, namely those who do not have to work to pay their bills, are truly free to decide whether to work, what work to do, where to work, when to work and how to work.

## Spiritual way to happiness and money

Happiness is a choice. We can choose happiness in any situation. If we actually live this idea, it can produce amazing results. Our happiness, or lack of it, is a choice we make every minute of every day in every situation. We can choose happiness at any moment in time. It's a choice we make in every situation. We can choose happiness in any situation. Try putting it into practice and we might just be amazed. At some point, we have all the money we need to have all the experiences we desire. When we reach that point, we have to question the value of spending our life and energy earning more.

- We only need one bed to sleep in, one chair to sit in and it doesn't take a lot of money to buy these things.

- World travel, considered a luxury by many, can be purchased for a reasonable price. The more luxury we buy when traveling, the more insulated we become from the experience we seek from travel in the first place. There's an efficient budget for traveling that avoids unnecessary hardship without insulating us from the country we came to visit.

- It doesn't take a lot of money to buy a good bicycle or backpack, but it does take time, health and freedom to enjoy bike trips and backpacking adventures.

- If travel and adventure isn't your passion, but arts and crafts are, then the same rule applies. It doesn't take a lot of money to pursue your artistic goals, but it does take time and health.

- Close, personal relationships cost very little to nurture, but they do require time to cultivate.

The message is quite clear: the stuff that is really important in life for happiness and fulfilment doesn't cost a lot of money. Happiness isn't the exclusive area of the wealthy. In fact, study after study has shown there's very little relationship between happiness and wealth once your income rises above miserable poverty. The reason is simple: unnecessary luxury is no substitute for a quality life experience. The spiritual approach is to think about ourselves not in terms of what we are worth or what we have, but who we are. What is our purpose as humans? According to the Zen way of living our purpose as humans is to 'be.' What does that mean? It means to be present in the moment. It also means to be grateful and in calibration with where our bodies and minds are at one time. If we are present in the moment, we aren't thinking about the past. We are not thinking of our mistakes; we do not have any guilt; we are not angry about anything. We are also not thinking about the future or its outcomes and failures. If we do not think of the future, we will not be anxious; we will have no fears and nothing to stress about. Most of our stress, anxiety and unhappiness about money comes from thinking about our past mistakes and the harm done to us, and also unnecessarily worrying about all the uncertainties of the future. Our past and future selves deprive our present selves of happiness when we allow ourselves to get deflected by these negative thoughts. Happiness comes from within. Material things or money cannot buy us happiness.

Money may not buy us happiness, but it does help us lead a comfortable life. If we have money, we don't have to worry about the food on our table, the clothes we wear, the house we live in and the bills we get at the end of the month. So clearly, it's easier to be in the Zen state of being; it certainly does help if our bills are taken care of. Money takes care of a lot of things in life. It certainly, and surely does help; however, it is not essential to happiness. Beyond a certain point, money will not help us be happy.

We will always find people around us who have very little money. How are they happy? This is because they have a good relationship with money, which is not dependent on who they are. They do not compare themselves with anyone. And they do not worry about their future or about things that are not in their control. They are sure they will always have enough for their needs. They are absolutely fine with who they are and where they are. They do not believe that having bigger houses and fancy cars is in any way going to revolutionise their life and expunge all their problems. It is not money that has power over them, they are the masters of their money. Also, they are not intimidated by money.

We believe that if we earn enough money or purchased that new iPhone, that we will be truly happy. But the joy doesn't last long, and we're back in a loop of desiring again. This is what causes us suffering. To be happy, we need to look inside ourselves. We don't need to grasp onto things around us in an attempt to find comfort and happiness from them. True inner peace comes from letting go of those attachments.

# *Chapter V*

## **Understand your Money and Mood Patterns**

————◆————

Working out our habits and thought patterns around money is a good thing to know. It could help us to know to think about things we want to work on.

- Think about the times we spend or save money and why.

- Think **about what aspects of dealing with money make our mental health worse**. Is it attending appointments, opening envelopes, confrontation or being misunderstood? Or is it something else?

- It could help to **keep a diary of our spending and our mood**. Try and record what we spent and why. Record how we were feeling before and afterwards too. This could help us work out any triggers or patterns.

When we understand more about what's happening in our life, we can think about what might help. Sometimes, just being aware of these patterns can help us feel more in control. For example, these are some common ways money and mental health can affect each other:

- Certain **situations might trigger feelings of anxiety and panic** e.g., talking to our bank. Or we might feel very anxious about a decision to spend money, even when we can afford it.

- If we're feeling low or depressed, we **may lack the motivation to take care of our finances**. It might not feel worth it.

- Spending may give us a brief high, so we might **overspend to feel better.**

- Going through a period of mania may lead to some **impulsive financial decisions**.

- If a mental health problem affects your ability to work or study that might have an **impact on your income.**

- Being in debt can cause **constant feeling** of anxiety.

- Worrying about money can lead to sleep issues.

- Money problems can **impact our relationships** and social life. You might feel lonely.

- We might not be **able to afford essential things** we all need to feel well. This might be house, food, water or medical emergencies.

**Avoid overspending when unwell**

Here are some tips that people have found helpful.

- **Confiding in someone we trust** about our triggers and warning signs so they can help us.

- **Giving our cards to someone else** or putting them somewhere difficult to access.

- Making it more difficult to spend money online by not **saving our card details into websites.** Search for free online tools to limit online spending.

- **Finding ways to delay purchasing.** We could tell ourselves, "I will buy this tomorrow if I still feel like it then." We could take photographs of the things we want or write them down in a wish list (on paper or phone). This might feel reassuring.

- **Distracting ourselves** with something else that makes us feel good. Going for a walk, calling a friend or watching something that we enjoy.

- **Telling our bank** that we have a mental health problem so they can take this into account. They may be able to add a note to our file to look out for unusual spending.
- Some people find it helpful to **avoid credit cards.**

**Share your worries**

Sharing our worries with someone we trust can be a relief. But it isn't always easy. Here are some people who might be able to help.

• **A trusted friend or family member.** Try and choose a quiet moment when the other person isn't distracted. It can sometimes help to make notes first or even write everything in a letter.

• **A support worker or health professional.**

• **Students** might find it helpful talking to their **teachers**. They may be able to help them apply for extra grants.

**Money worries connected with relationships**

Money can put a strain on relationships for lots of different reasons.

• We may find it hard to talk to our partner, friends or family about our debt or spending.

• We may be tempted to borrow money from people, but then have problems paying the money back. Or we may have lent money to someone else and feel worried about asking for it back.

• Speaking to housemates and friends about paying their way can sometimes feel stressful.

# Chapter VI

## Fear or Love: Your Dominant Emotion Towards Money

———◆———

**Fear of money**

Many of us fear not having enough money. There are plenty of places and times where this is an absolutely legitimate fear — after losing a job, when we've had an illness or death in the family or after realising that we have made a bad investment.

We live in times of materialistic excess. At times, we have a chronic, yet unfounded worry about not having enough money. At such times, fear is in the driver's seat of these choices. At such times, we avoid making choices that could lift us up, for we have a deep-rooted fear of money. We are afraid that we may not have enough for our difficult times. We are afraid of losing it. We have multiple fears and insecurities. We fear we may lose our job and not be able to pay our bills. We have fears of theft, of becoming an online fraud victim and so on and so forth. All such fear causes a lot of stress and anxiety. We are even scared of shopping online or of using cards.

When our basic needs for self-esteem and self-respect are not met, we give up easily, blame others, strive for less and mostly do not succeed in achieving our goals.

We allow fear to control our decisions without even realising it. A lot of times we get these fears for reasonably valid reasons. Money is important for our existence in a way that we are dependent on it, therefore we cannot take it casually. It's natural for us to have anxiety and get stressed in matters pertaining to money. Some of us are naturally more prone to becoming nervous and have misgivings related to our livelihood. While some us can take these things more casually. We have no apprehension as far as money is concerned.

Certain fears are ingrained in us since childhood. We grew up listening to our parents and elders to telling us to be very, very cautious with money. This develops a negative and fear-based mindset, and when we get into adulthood, we have this inbuilt fear of money.

When fear is our starting point, it results in us becoming greedy. Our concern is: what if our resources dry up? What will we leave for our children? All of modern society is fear-driven, which is detrimental. It can have a lasting harmful effect. We need to pay attention to our thoughts related to money. We need to be aware that fear dominates our money-related actions.

Chrometophobia (also called chrematophobia) is the intense fear of money. Both the words originate from Greek chermato, meaning money and phobos meaning a deep aversion, dread or fear.

Money is a necessity of life. However, to a person suffering from chrometophobia, dealing with money is extremely difficult. The phobia naturally affects one's daily life as shopping or working, traveling on buses and trains etc becomes very difficult. Some are only afraid of the corrupting power of money; some others might fear financial failures or the responsibility money brings.

## Do you love money?

When we are not fearful of something, we love it. We trust; we are sure this will not leave us — it will always be there. Love is acceptance; it is unconditional. Love doesn't worry about the past or the future.

We all need money because to live on the earth one requires money. Money in itself is not evil. It is the love of money that is evil. What is the difference between one who loves money and the one who does not? Is the one who loves money willing to do anything to make money without considering the morality involved in it? The love of money is evil and the end is disastrous, too. Despite the negative consequences of loving money, why do people still love money?

People who love money have the goal of becoming very rich. In fact, everybody knows that there is much to gain in this world if you are a rich man. The rich man, inevitably, becomes famous, makes a lot of friends and get away with a lot of things. He is well-praised and his faults are overlooked. The poor do not come any close to enjoying these privileges. That is why some people have given themselves to the love of money, hoping to become rich.

The body needs good food, shelter, clothes, comfort, good health service, etc. All these things are necessities that we all need to survive. The amount of money you have to your name decides the quality and the quantity of the necessities you have access to. A good example is that although both the wealthy and the poor eat daily, the quality and quantity of their food differ. Everyone loves money and will do anything to have more of it. Money promises a good standard of living for you to enjoy good food, decent shelter and quality health service.

Life comes with responsibilities for all, both young people and adults. But adults have financial responsibilities in addition. They need to pay the bills and fees and cater to their families. Sometimes, they have ageing parents to take care of. And, in most parts of the developing world, a person might be the breadwinner of an entire extended family. Hence, most adults are under pressure to bring money home due to the heavy financial burden they bear. Failure to fulfil these financial responsibilities comes with a series of many other problems. In a bid to meet financial responsibilities, many resort to the love of money. That is to say, they are willing and ready to use any shady means to make money, without considering the morality of it or the consequences thereof.

To love money is not about accumulating hordes of cash or obsessing over money. It's about loving yourself enough to produce the money you deserve, loving your work so you can more easily and happily generate wealth, and being a more loving person so that other people will be attracted to you and to whatever ideas, products or services you offer.

Love is the most powerful emotion human beings feel, and emotion has a lot to do with the results you get in life. There are probably a lot of millionaires who don't love money, but the ones who seem to be happiest and most fulfilled — creatively, personally, in business and in terms of making a difference in the world — exude their love and passion for what they do and the success they achieve. When we say they love money, it doesn't mean they lust after it or are even motivated by it. They do what they do because they love doing it, and other people — who are after all, the source of all our money — are attracted to that positive energy, and therefore are happy to give them lots of money. Super wealthy people like the late Steve Jobs, Richard Branson, Oprah, Jeff Bezos of Amazon and so on are driven by their love for what they do. They don't hate money or think it's an evil force — they enjoy the fruits of their labour, and they love everything about what they do in the world, include creating great wealth.

The love of money can never be satisfied. It is a hopeless love that always desires more. It is a wasted energy. And more than that, it keeps us, our attitude and our actions in bondage.

Where there is love of money, there is no freedom.

• **The love of money exhausts us**. Either we are thinking about how to create it, make it, grow it or save it, the fascination to earn more and more appropriates our most important and limited resource: time.

• **The love of money depletes our energy**. It requires constant, continual attention. After all, no opportunity to acquire more can ever be wasted.

• **The love of money annihilates our values.** When the love of money is present in our lives, we become different people. The passion for money is a trap that quickly swallows our heart convictions and causes us to engage in behaviours we would otherwise avoid.

• **The love of money fuels competition**. By definition, the love of money requires us to desire what others already possess. For us to gain more, others must part with theirs. The world quickly becomes a zero-sum game dominated by jealousy and envy.

• **The love of money limits our potential**. We can never become greater than that which we most desire. When the acquisition of money becomes our greatest goal in life, we can never become greater than the balance in our bank account. And that's a shame—we have so many greater things to offer this world.

• **The love of money attracts the love of money.** Our lives will naturally attract like-minded people. When we love money, we attract others who love money. And the more reinforcement we receive from those around us, the more natural the emotion becomes.

• **The love of money destroys other loves**. The love of money causes many to sacrifice their true passions and desires just to acquire more of it. It has truly killed many a passionate dream. To determine if the love of money has killed your dreams, answer this question, *"If the need for money were not a factor, what would I be doing today?"*

How then do we move beyond the desire to acquire more? While entire books have been written on this subject, let me throw out a few thoughts just to get you started toward freedom from the desire to acquire:

1. **See money only as a tool to move through life.** At its core, money is a bartering tool. It saves us from making our own clothes, tools, and furniture. Because of currency, we can spend our days doing

what we love and are good at. In exchange, we receive money to trade with someone else who uses their gift to create something different. That's the purpose of money. And if we have enough to meet our needs, we shouldn't commit the rest of our day to acquiring more.

2. **Be content with poverty or great wealth.** I know poor people who live in complete contentment and I know rich people who are further from contentment today than when they were poor. Our possessions do not lead to contentment. Our attitude does. And if the love for money limits freedom, contentment is the pathway to it.

3. **Avoid debt.** A lender is a slave to his creditor. Spending more money than we earn will always result in bondage to another. If we cannot get out from under the weight of debt, find some help.

4. **Learn to share.** Sharing our possessions with others benefits both the borrower and the lender. So, be a lender…and be a borrower.

5. **Remember that money comes and money goes.** Like the tides of the ocean, money rolls in and money rolls out. Sometimes, there is money left over at the end of the day and sometimes there is not enough. That is the very nature of money. Do not fear its cycles. Welcome them.

## Staying wealthy

There is plenty of material available on how to become rich. There are multiple ways to become wealthy. However, the difficult part is how to stay wealthy. Getting money is one thing. Keeping it another. Money success can be summarised in one word, 'survival.' Getting money and keeping money are two entirely different skills. To get money, we need to be optimistic and open to taking risks. To keep money, we need a fear of taking risks. Whatever we have made may vanish fast. We will have to be frugal and also accepting of the fact that some of what we have made may be because of luck. We should have fear and paranoia to survive. We can't afford to rest on past laurels.

We should have the mentality to survive; this should be the basis of our strategy to retain our riches. We need to know and accept that one year of growth will never show much progress, but 10 years can make a significant difference and 30 years may create something  extraordinary. However, getting and keeping that extraordinary growth requires surviving all the unpredictable highs and lows that we all go through over time.

To survive is a skill and we should be able to acquire it. Planning is an important tool of surviving strategy. Financial and investment planning are critical because they let us know whether our current actions are within the realm of reasonable. But very few plans survive their first encounter with the real world. A plan is useful if it can survive reality. A good plan has to be true; it is prepared for a future filled with uncertainty and unpredictability. It allows room for error. Many plans fail not because they had faults, but because they were mostly right in situations that required things to be right. We must always keep room for error; this is called margin of safety.

With planning, survival needs a little bit of sensible optimism as well. This means to have a belief that the odds are in our favour, and over a period of time things will even out to good outcome. The idea that something can grow in the long run, no matter how difficult it is on the way, is how things work in life. What is required is short-term paranoia to see us through long-term optimism.

# *Chapter VII*

## Money EQ

———◆———

Our emotional reaction to money is significant and essential to understand our relationship with money. This is known as money EQ, which includes how we receive, enjoy and share our money and also how confident we feel about money.

Our relationship with money grows and develops in a certain fashion. If we can ascertain the money pattern of our personality, we can have a healthier relationship with money. First, we need to find our present situation with money and determine how we got there. We will have to explore the past history of our family. Explore stories about our parents and perhaps our grandparents as well. Exploring our roots is important to understand ourselves to a greater extent. If we have a greater understanding of our descent, it becomes easier to reprogram our mindset, values and beliefs.

Our emotions are very important when it comes to handling of money. Most money mistakes we make are due to our emotional state. To make good money-related decisions, we need to be emotionally mature to handle our decisions rationally and sensibly, and not be reactionary in our approach. When we are responsible and sensible, only then can we make good decisions related to money. One way to do this is to become aware of our inherent nature and personality type.

When we think about money, several emotions crop up. Our reactions to money generally come from our subconscious. These can have a major impact on our relationship toward money and our feelings for money. And can limit the way we experience life.

## Money belief system

There is a reason why successful people are successful and unsuccessful people are unsuccessful. It depends on how we think about work and money. It determines our wealth and not our fate. One should have positive feelings towards money as it is our attitude towards our job and finances that gives our life a direction. If we are filled with anger, resentment, competitiveness and jealousy, we will get these things back from life.

We all have observed the patterns of our parents while growing up, and that is the only way we know. This is the pattern that governs our relationship with money. This is the manner in which we understand finances. Ideally, we should all learn and know what we feel about money, and know the reasons that helped us shape our feelings towards money.

We are never consciously taught about money,

how to handle it or how to take care of it. Still, in our subconscious we all have a certain pattern in the way we think about money or our habits related to money. We have consciously or unconsciously gathered this pattern from our parents and others around us or from the circumstances or experiences during our childhood. Early in our lives, we get conditioned to get money in a certain way. Many of us are conditioned to think about conservative ways only to earn money like the usual 10-to-5 jobs. Others may be conditioned to feel safe in the security of a government jobs, with the security of a fixed income right till the last day of their lives. They do not feel secure without a fixed monthly salary. However, if for some reason, they lose their job, they can only think of finding another job. They will not look or think of having any alternative ways of making money. We are still weary of exploiting unconventional (but legal and fair) methods of making money, since we are not very comfortable with taking financially risky decisions. For example, a hardcore investor would be comfortable leading a life without a job, but a person who is risk-averse will not take chances in life and not be willing to risk losing a secure lifestyle. Such people do not know how to make their money work for them.

Such people have been groomed to live in security. They have been taught to lead a simple and secure life. Such people do not aspire for more. They are okay living average, routine lives. They do not aspire to achieve more.

To lead a life of abundance, we should experience happiness when we think of money. You should actually feel joy at the physical touch of money. We should be able to smell its exuberance and not keep it tightly bundled up in our innermost pockets. We should not dread thinking or talking of money.

We need to discover what is our money paradigm and rewrite the parts that are working against us. It is possible to rewrite whatever pattern we have grown up with. We do not have to keep following the patterns our parents lived with; we can revise it.

We can always improve our relationship with money. We can better it and mould it the way we want. We will be required to heal our past relationship with money. We should have a feeling of gratefulness. We should feel we have enough to give away. Although the highest form of wealth is the ability to wake up every morning and say, "I can do whatever I want to." People want to become wealthier to make themselves happier. Everyone is happy for a different reason. However, there is one common factor that makes people happy—it is that people want to control their lives. We all want to be able to do what we want to do, and when we want to do it. This is greatest outcome of money. To be able to control one's life gives positive feelings about life. Control over doing what we want, when we want and the people we want in our life is actually what we seek as ultimate success.

Money gives us control over our time. A small amount of wealth means we will have the ability to take leave when we are sick without impacting our bank balance. People who do not have this luxury know what it means.

If we have a little more, we can wait for a good job even if we were laid off. This can have great impact on our life. This means that we have enough emergency funds and can wait for the job of our choice.

Using our money to buy time and options has a lifestyle benefit very few things can compete with. We like to feel like we are in control. When we are forced to do something, we feel disempowered because we didn't make the choice. Someone else did it for us.

A healthy relationship with money will bring us a sense of peace. Beware that it is a delusion that having more money will make us happy or solve all your problems. The truth is the richer we get, the more complex life becomes. We get more stressful as we have more work-related pressures. We will buy a bigger home when we have more money; we will have to work harder to pay the EMIs and so on and so forth. Our expenses increase just as our income does. Our life style keeps getting more expensive. So eventually, as our salary increases, we are still not left with much money at the end of the month.

If we get into that loop of wanting more, it takes away our ability to recognise what is actually most important in our life. When our work is doing well, we get addicted to the excitement. We go on playing as if in a game, and we start living in the illusion that our worth as a human is going up with each achievement. This game never ends because we keep wanting more and more.

If we genuinely want to be free of our money-related worries, we will have to look deep into our relationship with money in the past. We have to look into the causes of our fears. We will have to find out why we are controlled by money. We will be required to look for our personal patterns with money. We may be carrying negative emotions about money with people we were close to.

We carry a whole lot of memories, both good and bad, about money. Depending upon our patterns, money may arouse different emotions within us. Some people may feel happy thinking of money, whereas others may feel pain and confusion. For some, it may be a cause of anger, agony or distress. Our beliefs are formed when we are very young, like we talked about earlier, they are hidden deep within our subconscious. Later in life, they impact our dealings and decisions pertaining to money. All our lives we follow these imprints that shape our personality.

# *Chapter VIII*

# Relationship with Money

————•————

Money. No matter how you slice it, is a highly charged topic that can trigger all kinds of emotions. It may feel odd to think about having an 'emotional relationship' with money. Money or finances feel so 'practical.' On the other hand, looking at money and how it shows up for you can be extremely revealing to understand your feelings, behaviours and the impact it has on your relationships.

We have emotional relationships with many things—with work, our significant other, children, pets, sports teams, music, places or social issues we support. Why not money? How we feel about things tends to define how we interact with them. Our feelings project our values onto others, and in doing so affects how we relate to them as individuals.

## Common ways we think about money

We are all familiar with some of the most common ways in which we think about money. Some people are very careful, unwilling to spend money on anything unless it's absolutely necessary (money under the pillow concept). Some people love to spend money even when it might be a good idea to slow down a little and save. Many are somewhere in the middle, spending and treating themselves at times, and saving at others.

## How does this happen?

How do people develop these different relationships with money? As with most questions on the subject of emotions, the answer can often be traced back to how we were raised and our history with money throughout our lives. How did it show up for us as children, with our parents or caregivers? How did it reveal itself over time as we grew up and became adults? What experiences did we have that may have impacted our emotional relationship with money? We tend to develop our ideas around money from the people with whom we grew up, usually our parents or caregivers, and from experiences that have impacted us along the way.

The impact of how we were raised with money can cause us to model those same behaviours or do the exact opposite. If our parents were very careful with money or lived during the Great Depression, we might do the same thing. Or, because they want to provide their children with opportunities and material items they could never have themselves, they may overindulge or spend more than they should.

On a deeper level, as individuals, we all have our own emotional relationship with money, yet we are often wholly unaware of this and of our ability to abuse this within our relationships. We project meaning onto money, loading it with feelings around security, control, power, co-dependence and independence.

I have worked with couples where conflict can arise if one partner values their independence highly and projects this through their need for financial freedom, whereas the other wants to integrate resources and feels more secure when finances are co-mingled or even co-dependent. Some people need to feel in control of every single transaction whereas their partner may be completely disinterested in this level of detail. This can ignite intense frustration within the relationship.

Similarly, relational significance can come into play where we act out our roles reflecting a parent-child relationship, with one role being the parent or provider, and the other being the one who is provided for. The role of provider can have significant emotional implications for care giving and vice-versa, thus feeding into our sense of emotional security.
Unresolved past issues relating to money can also impact current relationships. For example, those who have had abusive relationships with their parents around money, or past traumatic relationships with a narcissist where money was used for control and power, these experiences can dirty even the healthiest of new relationships. If hidden debt is an issue within a relationship or if

one partner is simply hiding finances and purchases from the other, these can often have the same impact on a relationship as an affair — keeping secrets, betrayal of trust, despair and abandonment.

**How can you fix this?**

This is where having an understanding of our emotional relationship with money can be particularly helpful. When we think of it in these terms, we can approach the subject as we would any other relationship issue — through making an effort to empathise with each other's feelings.

By talking honestly about how we feel about money, what money means to us, what money evokes within us (fear, anxiety, distrust or even reignition of past trauma) and taking the time to examine together where these feelings might originate, we can gain a genuine understanding of one another's perspective. From there, we begin to move towards making decisions that take both of these perspectives into account and approach the practical sides of this discussion — how to budget together, which items to prioritise, joint account or separate and so on — in a healthier manner.

Individual therapy is a good way to begin our inner conversation about money and help us gain a deeper insight into our behaviours. Then, if we enter couples counselling, we can begin to better understand each other's perspectives and how to communicate with each other about money.

## Re-define your relationship with money

Once we have a clearer picture of where we fall on the scarcity-to-abundance spectrum, we can begin to ask: "What do I need to do to be in a state of ease in relation to money?"

For us to be in a state of ease with money, we:
  a) read finance-oriented books to develop confidence,
  b) get a financial advisor to feel extra-confident,
  c) begin to relax about money,
  d) decide to make a conscious choice to be non-judgmental whenever we chose to spend or not spend,
  e) began trusting that there's enough money to go around the world.

As a result, our relationship is less stressful when it comes to money.

## Set ground rules

When it comes to sensitive topics like money where people are bound to have some differences and to even trigger each other without knowing it, it's best to set some ground rules.

1. Remember that you're on the same side, even if you disagree.

2. Believe that your partner is doing what he/she thinks is best for both, even if it's not best for you.

3. Be interested in their perspective, even if don't understand at first.

4. Stop the conversation if it's getting too heated, even if you just want to prove yourself right, and agree to reconvene the discussion.

5. Don't try to manipulate your partner because that won't result in authentic resolution, even if you think it will give you a temporary solution.

6. Be responsible for your own happiness — if you need something, ask with zero expectations in return.

It may not be easy, but you can do it if you keep these ground rules in mind.

## Talk about your ideal lifestyle and where finances fit in

Begin with the end in mind. What are your long-term individual financial and life goals? Give yourself permission to dream big. What are your collaborative financial and life goals (e.g., kids, travel, home, school, transportation, fitness and lifestyle, owning your own business, etc.)? No matter the size of your dreams, review these goals together to see: (1) where you're aligned, (2) where you might want to make compromises and (3) where you can invite more abundance.

Once you have the end in mind, think strategically about where your relationship and finances are today in relation to where you want them to be, then set a phased lifestyle plan for moving forward.

Whether you decide to follow a strict budget, to avoid putting yourself in situations where you'd be tempted to spend carelessly, or to focus purely on abundance, make sure the system you use is clear for both of you.

# *Chapter IX*

## Financial Abundance through the Four Pillars of Money

––––•––––

The best way to achieve real change is to create a balance between these four pillars:

1. **The practical pillar of money** – using, managing and understanding money in the world today
2. **The value pillar of money** – understanding what value money brings to one's life and what it allows us to do
3. **The inner pillar of money** – our beliefs and unconscious understandings about money
4. **The spiritual pillar of money** – how money is part of our consciousness and the importance of healing our money stories

The first pillar is the **practical pillar** —managing our money on a practical level is the first step to financial abundance.

This allows us **to clear our mind of the worry and fear that our current situation may be causing,** or at the very least, the lack of clarity around what our situation actually is. In this way, we achieve more balance and that's an essential step in the right direction.

The second pillar is the **value pillar**—what value will money bring to our life?

Often, we think of money in terms of how much we want. But a far more powerful way is to **understand what value it will bring to us**— what is it we truly want in our life that money can help us have or do. Then, instead of chasing money, we're building a life vision and money becomes the tool to help us do that.

The third is the **inner pillar**—how do we feel and act around money?

Our beliefs control our behaviours and govern how we react to the experiences we have. We develop our habits from repeated behaviours.

So, if we have some stinking thinking around money, beliefs that don't support our quest for financial freedom, then there's a good chance that we're unconsciously engaging in behaviours that are sabotaging our success.

And finally, the **spiritual pillar**—our spiritual connection to money. Most of us see money as outside of us, something we have no control over. Sometimes, we see it as a 'necessary evil.' But actually, money is only the tool and how we use it is deeply connected to us and who we are on a spiritual level too. So, it's important to recognise the connection between all of ourselves and money.

As soon as we see it as something 'out there' that we have no influence over or connection with, we see it as separate from us. But in reality, it's not. Our money, and money in general, is intrinsically linked to our consciousness, and, just like anything else in our life, how we use it and feel about it has an impact on our experience of it.

# *Chapter X*

## Summing Up

———◆———

Money affects our attitudes, our feelings and our behaviour. And all of these three dimensions merge and link in various ways. Our relationship with money is rich and complex.

We acquire our financial knowledge and develop our attitudes towards money by way of financial socialisation.

Always take some time to notice how and when we spend money. What are our patterns—what motivates us to buy things? Do we shop impulsively? What are our triggers? We might want to start a spending diary to track our habits for a month to get a better idea. Having a better understanding of how and why we spend money.
Money is essential to meet some of our basic human needs, such as food and safe shelter. It allows us access to services that promote well-being, such as health and child care. If we can create some savings, we feel more secure. But money is not necessary for some of our other fundamental needs.

Money is not everything. It does not define us for who we are. It is just a mechanism to accomplish what matters to us, our goals in life. **We're not just a number and never let other people tell you otherwise.** We are who we choose to be. Money just helps us along the path.

We can't constantly bash ourselves up for spending an extra dollar by accident. It's so important to know that our self-worth is not just determined by our net worth. We all need to do this better. We need to celebrate wins and when we make a mistake, we can forgive ourself for it. This can be applied to any topic. Accidents happen, don't judge, don't feel ashamed.

Some economists think that money gives us subsistence, protection / security, affection, understanding, participation, leisure, creation, identity/meaning, freedom and transcendence. If you think about it, you can see that meeting some of these needs requires very little money.

We can meet our deepest needs for affection, understanding, belonging and identity through our relationships, pursuit of the purpose of life, spirituality, and our connection with nature.

Spending money on material goods doesn't bring lasting satisfaction. But there are ways that money can make us happier:

- Spending money on others
- Buying experiences, not material goods
- Creating more time in your life

We tend to compare our income with others and are only satisfied if it is higher. If we are offered a raise, but so is everyone else, we are less satisfied.

This is not limited to money. If we win a race, we will initially be elated, then begin to compare ourselves to someone who is even better — someone who won a bigger race.

Comparing ourselves to others and focusing on income is a never-ending exercise, and it only makes sense to make a deliberate effort to come out of it. Set aside time to reflect upon what you like and respect about yourself — without comparing with other people. Focus on how you have improved or grown without worrying about how you rank. Take satisfaction in how hard work and experience has developed your skills.

Take a good look at your budget. While humans have a tendency to adjust expectations upward as income goes up, we can consciously change that. Instead of wanting more expensive things and more of them, we can choose to save new income. Instead of buying things, we can give ourselves the security of having enough money.

Credit cards can lead us into temptation because they separate the pain of payment from the pleasure of purchasing something new.
Saving works the other way — we have the pain of less money to spend right up front, and don't necessarily see the pleasure of having money to live

on in the future. So, we need to find ways to increase the incentive to save.

Unemployment is one of the most difficult situations we face. It can be devastating to a family's financial security on many levels. A loss of a job not only impacts income, but brings other major losses: social connections, status and the intrinsic satisfaction of using our skills.

Recognising this can help us enlist strategies to minimise losses. For instance, we can search for other ways to use our skills and feel productive while we are looking for a job. Make sure we connect with our social network for support throughout.

We work harder and longer so we can eventually have the freedom to do what we want when we want. The paradox is that we are giving up the very thing we say we want in order to have it sometime in the future. Often, this never happens because we never feel we have enough money to actually slow down and enjoy the very thing we think we're working to have.

We often put ourselves under such pressure in the pursuit of more money that our health suffers. The Dalai Lama is quoted as saying *"... [man] sacrifices his health in order to make money. Then he sacrifices money to recuperate his health..."*

Often, we spend months, even years, **doing something we don't enjoy**—all in the name of money. The idea is to suffer for a short time and then live it up once we get to the level of income we want. But usually, it doesn't work that way because there is never 'enough,' there's **always one more level to get** to before we can quit and 'be happy.'

So, what do we trade for money? **What insights have we had about our relationship with money?** Taking time to uncover how we feel about and behave around money, not to mention what we trade for it, is a big step towards changing how we see money and therefore, how it works in our life.

Making it a priority to develop a better understanding of our relationship with money will build strong a foundation to work from when looking to improve our financial situation.

Show care about where our money's going by creating a budget, learn more about it, such as how to invest it wisely and work on any issues that come up. This will change our vibration around money and we'll find that it will begin to flow into our life far more easily than we ever believed it could.

So, very simply, if we want to attract money into our bank—we need to treat it like a good friend rather than an enemy and get excited about what we're going to use it for.

**Financial abundance is something that everyone aspires to. The trouble is that often the idea of managing money sounds so boring, but it's necessary.**

One of the most important values to anyone who is genuinely a free spirit is freedom. But if money is a constant worry, or if we're always being held back because of a lack of finances, we will never experience true freedom.

The good news is that even though financial abundance is partly about looking after our money, it's not all about budgets and number crunching.

**Tips to shift to a wealth mindset**

Tip #1 - List your innermost thoughts and feelings around money

Making these changes to the way we live with our money is not really that difficult. We just need to be aware of the times when we shift away from feeling abundant and bring ourself back again, enjoy life and allow things to flow.

Because one thing is for certain—a wealth mindset is far easier to attain when we feel good, and will lead us to living life our way and thriving, with abundance that encompasses far more than just money.

**Having a wealth mindset is directly linked to living a life of abundance—which is our natural**

**state. But when it comes to money, often our thoughts lead us to finding lack rather than plenty.**

Of course, **abundance isn't all about money**. But because money seems to be something that we struggle with, that's what I want to talk about today.

Be honest, when we think about money — what is the first thing that comes to mind? Is it that there's plenty to go around and it's easy to get, or is it some version of there's never enough?

*"You can only become truly accomplished at something you love. Don't make money your goal. Instead, pursue the things you love doing, and then do them in a manner that people can't take their eyes off you."* Maya Angelou.

# REFERENCES

1. Twist, L.  The Soul Of Money : Transforming Your Relationship With Money and Life, New York : W.W.Norton , 2006.
2. Forbes July 6th 2020
3. Housel, Morgan : The Psychology of Money: Timeless Lessons on Wealth, Greed, and Happiness.
4. Harriman House Ltd. 2020.
5. Richards , Charles : The Psychology Of Wealth.: Understand Your Relationship With Money and Achieve Prosperity. McGraw Hill. USA 2012.
6. Dunn, Elizabeth and Norton, Michael :Happy Money : The New Science Of Smarter Spending.
7. One World Publisher . UK. 2013.
8. Honda ,Ken : Happy Money . John Murray Learning.2019.